D0838442

WHEN A NATION TURNS ITS BACK TO GOD

LIVING AS A **BIBLE-BELIEVING MINORITY**
in the UNITED STATES *of* AMERICA

PAUL CHAPPELL

First published in 2015 by Striving Together Publications, a ministry
of Lancaster Baptist Church, Lancaster, CA 93535. Striving Together
Publications is committed to providing tried, trusted, and proven
resources that will further equip local churches to carry out the
Great Commission. Your comments and suggestions are valued.

Striving Together Publications
4020 E. Lancaster Blvd.
Lancaster, CA 93535
800.201.7748
strivingtogether.com

Cover design by Andrew Jones
Layout by Craig Parker
Writing assistance by Monica Bass and Robert Byers
Research assistance by David Adams, Monica Bass, and Rick Houk

The author and publication team have put forth every effort to give proper
credit to quotes and thoughts that are not original with the author. It is not
our intent to claim originality with any quote or thought that could not
readily be tied to an original source.

ISBN 978-1-59894-306-1
Printed in the United States of America

Contents

A New Minority

I grew up in San Jose, California, during the age of the American sexual revolution and the free love movement.

In response to the moral upheaval, conservative Christians began concerted efforts not only to reach more people with the gospel, but also to speak to the moral issues in society and government. As a result, there was a resurgence of Christian values in society, that some of my early mentors referred to as a "moral majority." (In fact, in the 1980s, Dr. Jerry Falwell founded an organization by that name.) Others, too, organized rallies, wrote articles, got on Christian radio stations, and did everything they could to awaken the American people to the moral decadence of the culture and unite them around moral values.

But what I remember most of all during the late '60s, the '70s, and even the early '80s was the resurgence of evangelism among Baptist churches. Indeed, many churches launched aggressive, city-wide soulwinning ministries and began bus outreach to minister to underprivileged areas of their cities with the gospel. Many independent Baptist churches multiplied in size in a matter of a few years simply by seeing unchurched people come to Christ through their witnessing efforts.

Those were good days for Baptist churches—and, by extension, for thousands of communities around America as well. Many of those churches made dramatic differences in the communities in which they lived. And the combined effect of their labor led to a resurgence of moral values as Christians across America rose up in support of conservative leaders. Overall, moral issues came back in check and the

American people once again elected public officials with conservative moral beliefs.

But America has changed rapidly, hasn't she? In my lifetime, I've seen the rise and fall of the "moral majority." Today, immorality is not only rampant but also celebrated.

As Christians, the moral decadence of our culture may grieve us, but it shouldn't altogether surprise us. Second Timothy 3 describes the world in the days preceding the return of Christ as a world that is out of control morally, passionately pursuing that which is unnatural, and disregarding God with an unthankful spirit.

> *This know also, that in the last days perilous times shall come. For men shall be lovers of their own selves, covetous, boasters, proud, blasphemers, disobedient to parents, unthankful, unholy, Without natural affection, trucebreakers, false accusers, incontinent, fierce, despisers of those that are good, Traitors, heady, highminded, lovers of pleasures more than lovers of God;*—2 TIMOTHY 3:1–4

Just a few decades removed from the resurgence of the "moral majority," we see today what can only be described as a "moral minority" in America.

Gallup polls suggest that, whereas two decades ago, a large majority of Americans believed that homosexual unions should not be called "marriage," today, this belief is in the minority.[1]

Homosexuality isn't the only issue over which Americans have rejected God. But, as I'll highlight in chapter 2, I believe Scripture indicates that the promotion of the homosexual lifestyle is a tipping point for a nation as an expression of willful godlessness. Although some would suggest that issues such as homosexuality or same-sex marriage should be limited to the political or social spheres of discussion, I disagree. At its very core, human sexuality is a moral issue (not to mention a gift from God), and our current national attitude toward it reveals an ultimate rejection of God's design.

As of June 26, 2015— the date of the Supreme Court decision declaring same-sex marriage to be a constitutional right —America officially turned from God's definition of the family. Ultimately, our society has enthroned human desires over God's design.

This didn't happen overnight. We've heard the rumblings for years now. It began with the sexual revolution of the '60s when many rejected God's pattern for intimacy and relationships. (The Bible not only forbids homosexuality, but it forbids all sex outside of marriage [1 Corinthians 6:9–20, Hebrews 13:4].) Of course, in the '60s these types of initiatives were led by a relatively small number of counter-culture "rebels." But in the past couple of decades, corporate America jumped on the bandwagon.

AT&T was one of the early pacesetters, founding the first LGBT employee resource group in corporate America in 1987. LEAGE was formed to provide visibility to the goal of LGBT acceptance.[2] By the mid-'90s, Warner Bros. and Sony were offering health benefits to both members of same-sex partnerships, just as they would to married couples.[3] And Disney followed soon after.[4] Not to be left out, JP Morgan Chase used their already-active gay/lesbian network, Pride, to try to gain new clients.[5] In 2002 a host of companies—including Wells Fargo, American Airlines, American Express, IBM, Intel, JP Morgan Chase, and Motorola—founded the National Gay & Lesbian Chamber of Commerce to promote LGBT business interests.[6]

Then amazingly, churches got involved. As early as 1972, the United Church of Christ ordained gay clergy.[7] The Evangelical Lutheran Church followed in 2009[8] and the Presbyterian Church USA in 2011.[9] To be sure, these are churches which decades before had denied the core doctrines of the Bible and the Christian faith and, as such, are apostate churches.

Yet, to LGBT activists, the "church's" acceptance of homosexuality as merely an alternative lifestyle served their argument that churches who disagree are bigoted.

In more recent days, our military has actively enforced open acceptance of homosexuality. In June 2012, the Pentagon held a gay pride event, including a panel on "The Value of Open Service and Diversity."[10] (I'm not aware, however, of any military events that have been held to encourage the support of or respect for traditional families.)

Even among the general American public, there is increased pressure to embrace the homosexual movement as good, healthy, and right. Those who dare to believe otherwise or support another message— even privately with their own time or resources—may be ostracized and lose their jobs, as was the case with Brendan Eich, CEO of Mozilla,[11] and Kelvin Cochran, Fire Chief of Atlanta, Georgia.[12]

So much for "tolerance." It turns out that those calling for "tolerance" are the most intolerant of anyone who does not agree with and further their cause.

Yes, America as I knew it has changed. Today, Christians of all ethnicities who believe and practice the Bible are a minority group. And frankly, it will become more uncomfortable in the days ahead for Christians who believe what the Bible says and are willing to take a public stand for it.

To be very clear, I hate no one. I believe that every person is made in the image of God and thus deserves respect and dignity. I want every person to know the love of Christ, and the church which I am privileged to pastor works tirelessly to this end in our community. I trust that in the pages to follow, you'll not only hear my stand for biblical truth but will sense my concern and care for people to know Christ and the liberating power of the gospel.

There is a rise in America of people who interpret disagreement as bigotry and difference as intolerance. To these people, the acceptance of homosexuality is really not an issue of love, for they do not respect the freedom of those who disagree. It is an ideology that insists on dominance.

Take for instance the Religious Freedom Restoration Act (RFRA) of Indiana which Governor Pence signed into law. The law was designed to protect those who see same-sex marriage as a moral issue and would allow someone to cite religious convictions in their defense when sued by a private party.[13] The outcry against this law was so forceful it would lead one to wonder if the only rights to be protected are those of gays. The cities of Denver,[14] San Francisco,[15] and Washington D.C.[16] prohibited all public personnel from city-funded travel into the entire state of Indiana. The governor of Connecticut signed an executive order banning state employees from state-funded travel to Indiana.[17] Major companies, including Apple, Wal-Mart, Target, Pepsi, Marriott International, and Gap, all spoke in opposition to the bill.[18] Angie's List cancelled a $40 million headquarters expansion in Indianapolis.[19] The outcry was so strong that the Indiana governor eventually backed down.[20] And all that over a law to protect liberty.

Yes, I believe the days ahead for the religious liberty of Christians are tense. But take heart, while current events and recent developments are discouraging, our future as Bible-believing Christians isn't ominous. It's bright.

Look at the opening words to the Apostle Peter's epistle: "Peter, an apostle of Jesus Christ, to the strangers scattered throughout Pontus, Galatia, Cappadocia, Asia, and Bithynia" (1 Peter 1:1). Notice that Peter didn't address his letter "to those in power," but "to the strangers scattered." First-century Christians knew nothing of a "moral majority." They lived as strangers—aliens—in their own countries. In some cases, they were even far from home—"scattered" by persecution.

Throughout history, Christians have not always had sympathetic representatives in leadership. In fact, the religious freedom we enjoy in America has been largely unknown to any other nation at almost any other time in history. I love America for our heritage of freedom, and I desire to see it protected and prolonged. But I don't pin my hope for the future of Christianity to it.

As a Bible-believing minority in America today, we are those scattered as strangers throughout an unbelieving society. Based on our beliefs in God's Word, we are the minority in the workforce, community, government, and sometimes even our own families. We are as the Jews in Egypt and the Hebrew children in Babylon. And as such, we must live with loyalty to our God and teach our children to live with conviction.

The good news is—and there is much good news—Christianity not only *survives* repression; it *thrives* in such contexts.

Many of the greatest spiritual awakenings of history came in the darkest times. The Word of God is not bound—not by history, not by popular opinion, not by a rejecting culture. As we'll see in the pages ahead, we are entering some of the greatest opportunities to see God's redemption at work and to see Christ build His church.

Even so, many of us wonder, how did we get here as a nation? How did we as Christians suddenly find ourselves as strangers living in a country birthed to provide religious freedom? And more importantly, how do we make a difference for Christ?

We'll answer the first two questions in Part 1 as we describe the realities surrounding us today. And we'll answer the final question in Part 2 as we prescribe the biblical response modeled by first-century Christians.

Yes, we are strangers—a minority in a godless culture. But we are also victors—more than conquerors through Christ who loves us and who loves the people of the world in which we live.

PART ONE

The Reality of a Changing Culture

The king raised his knife high above the struggling animal bound below.

He hesitated. He did not question the wisdom of his choice—he had already set his course—but he felt for the approval of the crowd. Had he succeeded in gaining their acceptance? Had he maintained his political influence?

He plunged his knife, and the golden calf before him seemed to nod approval. Yes, this was the right choice for a changing culture. Why hold to the old places of worship and restrictions of the narrow minded? Why not add new places, times, and modes of worship? Why not include more leaders—and keep more followers in the process?

With that first sacrifice, Jeroboam turned a nation's face from the God of their fathers to new gods—gods that appealed to a culture of changing values and encouraged less restricted worship.

Whereupon the king took counsel, and made two calves of gold, and said unto them, It is too much for you to go up to Jerusalem: behold thy gods, O Israel, which brought thee up out of the land of Egypt. And he set the one in Bethel, and the other put he in Dan. And this thing became a sin: for the people went to worship before the one, even unto Dan. And he made an house of high places, and made priests of the lowest of the people, which were not of the sons of Levi. And Jeroboam ordained a feast in the eighth month, on the fifteenth day of the month, like unto the feast that is in Judah, and he offered upon the altar. So did he in Bethel, sacrificing unto the calves that he had made: and he placed in Bethel the priests of the high places which he had made.—1 Kings 12:28–32

As a tour guide in Israel pointed out to me, when Jeroboam offered his sacrifices, he literally had his back to Jerusalem. Even in his physical posture, he demonstrated that he had turned his *back to God.*

CHAPTER 1

The Record of Scripture

How did a nation that carved the words of Scripture into its stone monuments and inscribed "In God We Trust" on its currency come to the place where the Bible is openly scorned and its truth is disregarded?

How does *that* nation so reject the record of Scripture, that its highest court sets itself above and in opposition to the revealed Word of God (as the United States Supreme Court did in the June 26, 2015 verdict to grant constitutional rights to same-sex marriage)?

Departure from the truth does not happen suddenly. Our society did not wake up one day and jettison thousands of years of truth regarding marriage. Over time we've turned from a belief in absolute truth, and a belief that such truth is recorded in the pages of Scripture.

An Inerrant Source

At the very foundation of our belief in truth is an understanding of the nature of the Word of God. The Bible is not a collection of man's ideas and compiled ancient wisdom. It is the perfect Word of God, divinely inspired and preserved for us through the ages.

Second Timothy 3:16 says, "All scripture is given by inspiration of God, and is profitable for doctrine, for reproof, for correction, for instruction in righteousness." The psalmist tells us, "Thy word is true from the beginning: and every one of thy righteous judgments endureth for ever" (Psalm 119:160). Jesus prayed, "Sanctify them through thy truth: thy word is truth" (John 17:17).

God's Word is absolutely true and inerrant. If God says it, we can count on it. One author wrote, "Not only is the Bible inspired, but by means of this inspiration it is inerrant, or without error. Whatever God utters is the truth without error."[21] The Bible is accurate in everything that it presents, and we can have complete confidence in what it says. There are many who question the Word of God and claim to have found errors and contradictions. But the Bible, rightly understood and interpreted, never leads us wrong. Peter wrote, "We have also a more sure word of prophecy; whereunto ye do well that ye take heed, as unto a light that shineth in a dark place, until the day dawn, and the day star arise in your hearts" (2 Peter 1:19).

Rightly Dividing the Truth

Have people made claims that the Bible teaches something that is false? Of course. Have people misunderstood what the Bible says and been led into error as a result? Often. Many make fun of scriptural truth, twisting passages out of context to support errant views which they can then ridicule. This is why it is critical that we apply ourselves to learning first what the Bible says and then how it applies to our lives. Paul instructed Timothy, "Study to shew thyself approved unto God, a workman that needeth not to be ashamed, rightly dividing the word of truth" (2 Timothy 2:15).

One of the favorite tactics of biblical critics is to question a passage written in a different dispensation—a different time in history to a different group of people and for a different purpose. In other words, it is to pull a passage from the historic, biblical context in which it should be understood, superimpose it into a context for which it was not meant, and then point out that even Christians do not follow that teaching.

For example, in 2006, then-Senator Barack Obama said, "Whatever we once were, we are no longer just a Christian nation; we are also a Jewish nation, a Muslim nation, a Buddhist nation, a Hindu nation, and a nation of nonbelievers." Besides using "a Christian nation" in a historically inaccurate context (even as a self-proclaimed Christian nation, the United States of America has *always* included and protected the freedom of people of diverse religions), he ridiculed the Bible as he continued: "If we were to be a Christian nation...should we go with Leviticus, which suggests slavery is okay and that eating shellfish is abomination? How about Deuteronomy, which suggests stoning your child if he strays from the faith? Or should we just stick to the Sermon on the Mount—a passage that is so radical that it's doubtful that our own Defense Department would survive its application?"[22]

We do interpret the Bible literally, but we interpret it historically as well. For instance, God gave laws to the Israelites that were clearly written to them specifically during that time in their history. These laws were not given to the surrounding nations, nor were they moral laws. Scripture written in that context may not be directly applicable to people today.

God gave the Israelites His law in part to reveal His holiness. He also gave His law to protect them from diseases that were spread through lack of sanitation and ignorance concerning bacteria. To say that Scripture commands things that God did *not* indicate were binding to every group of people in every generation is misleading. (This would include the eating of shellfish as well as planting two crops in the same field.)

Another example that often comes up is the issue of slavery and the fact that biblical law allowed slavery among the Jewish people. It is important to note that the kind of slavery being talked about in the Old Testament is different than the slavery that existed in the United States. In Israel, slavery was usually for working off debts (more of an indentured servitude) and in all cases was regulated in ways that recognized the personhood of those in service. When we think of the word *slavery* today, we call to mind the brutal, inhumane, literal ownership of another person—in some cases even denying that they were fully human—

of past America. Slavery is a sad blight on our history—one that is in no way supported by Scripture. Rather, Scripture emphasizes that all people are made in the image of God and are worthy of respect and the right to freedom.[23] To claim that the Bible supports slavery in the sense we understand it, is either ignorant or misleading.

When conversing with those who scoff at the Bible, we must be aware of the historical, dispensational context of Scripture. Although all of Scripture is perfect and permanently enduring (Jesus said, "Heaven and earth shall pass away, but my words shall not pass away," Matthew 24:35), the simple reality is that not every command recorded was intended by God to be permanently binding in every generation. On the other hand, Scripture's instruction concerning marriage and sexuality are repeated throughout Scripture and are clearly given as the design of God for the entire human race.

Those of us who believe the Bible and are committed to honoring its teachings need to be ready to explain our position and face these objections.

But we should do so from a position of confidence because God's Word never fails. We may be opposed and attacked for believing the Bible, but we will never be in error if we are standing on what Scripture truly says. It is the inerrant, revealed truth of God.

Let's notice these truths in relation to one of the main cultural issues of our day—marriage and sexual relationships.

The Origin of Marriage

Marriage itself was God's idea—and a wonderful one at that! We find the origin of marriage in the Creation account of Genesis 1.

As God created the world, each day He looked at what He had made and saw it was good. Yet, after He created Adam, he saw a void: "And the LORD God said, It is not good that the man should be alone; I will make him an help meet for him" (Genesis 2:18). The reality is that God in His perfect knowledge saw that there was a need for companionship, love, and family in the human part of His creation.

God's solution to that need was to create a woman. "And the LORD God caused a deep sleep to fall upon Adam, and he slept: and he took one of his ribs, and closed up the flesh instead thereof; And the rib, which the LORD God had taken from man, made he a woman, and brought her unto the man" (Genesis 2:21–22). Lehman Strauss pointed out, "The first marriage was God's doing. Marriage was not a human idea but a divine institution."[24]

Because marriage is not a human idea, it is not up to man to decide what marriage is or what the terms of marriage are to be. Those are set by God Himself, and no human authority—no court, no judge, no president, no king, no congress—has the right to change it. The Supreme Court verdict overturning the laws of many states may change the legal definition of marriage in America, but it does not change the truth. Regardless of how the term "same-sex marriage" may be used, there is no such reality—marriage by God's definition is between one man and one woman.

Jesus Himself reiterated the definition of marriage as He quoted from Genesis 2: "And he answered and said unto them, Have ye not read, that he which made them at the beginning made them male and female, And said, For this cause shall a man leave father and mother, and shall cleave to his wife: and they twain shall be one flesh? Wherefore they are no more twain, but one flesh. What therefore God hath joined together, let not man put asunder" (Matthew 19:4–6).

Incidentally, those who oppose God's plan for marriage are not finished with expanding its definition. In his dissent to the Supreme Court decision legalizing same-sex marriage, Chief Justice John Roberts wrote, "It is striking how much of the majority's reasoning would apply with equal force to the claim of a fundamental right to plural marriage. If not having the opportunity to marry 'serves to disrespect and subordinate' gay and lesbian couples, why wouldn't the same 'imposition of this disability,' serve to disrespect and subordinate people who find fulfillment in polygamous relationships?"

Critics suggested that Chief Justice Roberts was being an alarmist, but just a few days after his statements, Nathan Collier, a Montana resident, applied for a marriage license to marry a second wife. He said he was inspired by the legalization of gay marriage. Collier stated, "It's about marriage equality. You can't have this without polygamy."[25]

When *marriage* becomes defined merely by the words *love, commitment,* or *dignity,* there's no telling where its elastic definition will end. One thing is for sure: there will be further efforts to expand the definition of marriage beyond what God has laid out.

This is why Bible-believing Christians must be prepared to scripturally define marriage—for ourselves, our children, our churches, and for unbelievers. But beyond defining marriage, we must be people who by example live out God's sacred purposes for marriage.

The Three-Fold Purpose for Marriage

God not only originated marriage, but He set up its operation. Throughout Scripture, we see at least three clear purposes for marriage.

Marriage is meant for future preservation of the human race. To the very first husband and wife, God said, "…Be fruitful, and multiply, and replenish the earth…" (Genesis 1:28). The fact is that a man and woman can have children while a same-sex union cannot. Although not every couple will or is able to have children, generally speaking, procreation is the natural result of marriage. Thus, even as God instituted marriage, He built into it the ability to preserve the family and the human race throughout the generations to follow.

Marriage is meant for restricted physical companionship. Physical intimacy is a wonderful thing, but the only place where God has designed for that legitimate desire to be fulfilled is within the bonds of marriage between one man and one woman. No others are ever to enter that relationship, which by God's design is only to begin at marriage. This truth contradicts many lifestyles today and even lifestyles in Bible times, but it is clear in the pages of Scripture. Hebrews 13:4 says, "Marriage is honourable in all, and the bed undefiled: but whoremongers and adulterers God will judge."

Marriage is meant to be a picture of Christ's relationship to the church. Because God's wisdom is so far beyond us, He gives us illustrations to help us understand who He is and how He works with us. The love of the husband for his wife and the obedience of the wife toward her husband is a model of the relationship Jesus wants to have with His church. "For we are members of his body, of his flesh, and of his bones. For this cause shall a man leave his father and mother, and shall be joined unto his wife, and they two shall be one flesh. This is a great mystery: but I speak concerning Christ and the church" (Ephesians 5:30–32).

Refer back to those three purposes, and you can see that the push for same-sex marriage directly attacks all three: A relationship between two men or two women does not produce children. It does not provide a legitimate setting for physical intimacy. And it does not picture the relationship between Christ and the church.

The objections raised against the Christian position are not really directed at us, but at God. The rebellion in the hearts of sinful people manifests itself by trying to destroy what God has created and replacing it with human substitutes. Every such effort is doomed to failure from the start.

The family that God designed is the bedrock of civilization. Our fortieth president, Ronald Reagan said, "There is no institution more vital to our nation's survival than the American family. Here the seeds of personal character are planted, the roots of public virtue first nourished. Through love and instruction, discipline, guidance, and example, we learn from our mothers and fathers the values that will shape our private lives and our public citizenship."

The truth of God's design and plan for marriage is eternal and unchanging, and we must resolve to defend and stand for that truth, no matter what is going on around us. For, as we will see next, the rejection of God's design is disastrous.

CHAPTER 2

The Rejection of a Nation

Although God is clear and consistent in revealing His truth, He does not force us to follow it. Indeed, the current events of our nation reveal the rejection of truth, as the majority of Americans have said, "We reject the revealed truth of God concerning marriage. We will not stand by it."

The United States of America is not the first nation to defy God and His plan. Throughout Scripture and history we see example after example of governments and people who turn their backs on

God—not because they do not *know* what He says, but because they do not want to *do* it.

Psalm 2:1–3 paints an accurate picture of man's rebellion toward God's rule: "Why do the heathen rage, and the people imagine a vain thing? The kings of the earth set themselves, and the rulers take counsel together, against the Lord, and against his anointed, saying, Let us break their bands asunder, and cast away their cords from us."

Today our nation's leaders often decide their positions, not based on unchanging truth or even personal convictions, but based on the general opinions of the electorate. In many instances, leaders are willing to reverse previously held positions—ones which they said they firmly believed—to adapt to the changing moods of the culture.

For example, a simple comparison of two quotes by President Barack Obama shows a complete capitulation on the issue of same-sex marriage. In a November 1, 2008 (three days before the presidential election) interview with MTV, Obama said, "I believe marriage is between a man and a woman. I am not in favor of gay marriage."[26] Four years later, President Obama told Robin Roberts on Good Morning America, "At a certain point, I've just concluded that for me personally, it is important for me to go ahead and affirm that I think same-sex couples should be able to get married."[27]

As we saw in the introduction, President Obama is not the only one who has changed position on same-sex marriage. So, what happened? Did the truth change? Did God decide to start accepting same-sex marriage because more Americans thought it was a good idea? Did something that has been known to be wrong for thousands of years suddenly become right? No. A nation that is actively rejecting God has elected leaders and appointed judges who desire to throw off the laws of God and go their own way.

A Pattern of Rejection

A pattern of national rebellion can be traced back through the pages of Scripture. We see it repeated throughout the nation of Israel's history, and we also see it—perhaps in a context more closely matched to our own—in first-century Rome. The process is spelled out for us in Romans 1. Read these verses, and notice the progression:

God revealed His truth: *"For the wrath of God is revealed from heaven against all ungodliness and unrighteousness of men, who hold the truth in unrighteousness; Because that which may be known of God is manifest in them; for God hath shewed it unto them"* (Romans 1:18–19).

God is generous in revealing His truth. He has given us Scripture. He has given us the laws of nature. And He has given us the human conscience. Only Scripture is the supernatural revelation of truth, but all three of these point to God's truth.

Yet, what has man done with God's truth? Rejected it.

Man resisted the truth: *"Because that, when they knew God, they glorified him not as God, neither were thankful; but became vain in their imaginations, and their foolish heart was darkened. Professing themselves to be wise, they became fools"* (Romans 1:21–22).

Men who are not willing to give God glory and thanks for all that He has done are on a foolish path. The end of that path is clear from the beginning, but they are so opposed to the truth that they don't care.

We know what the end result of rejecting God, through homosexuality and all other kinds of immorality, will be because we can read the pages of history and find out the fate of societies that have lowered the value of marriage. Yet we are headed down the path of ruin full speed ahead.

To legitimize his resistance of truth, man needs and turns to a new object of worship.

Man worshipped the creation rather than the Creator: *"And changed the glory of the uncorruptible God into an image made like to corruptible man, and to birds, and fourfooted beasts, and creeping things. Wherefore God also gave them up to uncleanness through the lusts of their own hearts, to dishonour their own bodies between themselves: Who changed the truth of God into a lie, and worshipped and served the creature more than the Creator, who is blessed for ever. Amen"* (Romans 1:23–25).

While we should take care of God's creation as He intended from the beginning, many people today have placed the world that God has created over God Himself. They weep over the killing of a lion while they reject the sanctity of human life. They worry about global warming while scoffing at the biblical warning of an eternity of burning fire that awaits.

Man perverted what was normal and right: *"For this cause God gave them up unto vile affections: for even their women did change the natural use into that which is against nature: And likewise also the men, leaving the natural use of the woman, burned in their lust one toward another; men with men working that which is unseemly, and receiving in themselves that recompence of their error which was meet"* (Romans 1:26–27).

Remember, it is *God* who gave us the gifts of marriage and sexual intimacy. Enjoyed as God ordained, they are pure and right and good. But when people reject God, they twist the good gifts which He has given and create a new normal.

Once people decide that God's way will not satisfy them, they will go to any length to try to fill the empty places in the human heart. But sin always produces diminishing results, meaning they have to go further and further, and their true needs are never met.

Man willfully forgot God: *"And even as they did not like to retain God in their knowledge, God gave them over to a reprobate mind, to do those things which are not convenient; Being filled with all unrighteousness, fornication, wickedness, covetousness, maliciousness; full of envy, murder, debate, deceit, malignity; whisperers, Backbiters, haters of God, despiteful, proud, boasters, inventors of evil things, disobedient to parents, Without understanding, covenantbreakers, without natural affection, implacable, unmerciful: Who knowing the judgment of God, that they which commit such things are worthy of death, not only do the same, but have pleasure in them that do them"* (Romans 1:28–32).

When a society reaches this level, there are almost no limits to what will be done or accepted. Not only does evil and immorality become widespread, but it is *celebrated*. Frequently those who speak out for the truth find themselves criticized or attacked.

In our day, we see this unfolding as elected officials march in gay pride parades, while Christian business owners that do not want to make cakes or take pictures for gay weddings are facing crippling fines. We see it as celebrities who have sex-changes are heralded as examples of courage while teenagers who remain morally pure are ridiculed.

Even in the aftermath of the June 2015 Supreme Court decision on gay marriage, we saw this played out as the mayor of New York City walked with two million people in an LGBT parade while a nearby priest was spat upon and Christians were denigrated.[28]

Once again, I remind you that this was the type of world that Paul, Peter, and the early church contended with in the first century. In Corinth, Ephesus, Rome, and other cities, evil, immoral practices were celebrated while good was condemned. So don't become discouraged by recognizing our culture's rejection of truth. But don't turn a blind eye either.

An Official Rejection

It's one thing for individual Americans or even the President to voice personal opinions that are contrary to God's Word. But it's another for a nation to formally state them as an official national position. This is what happened in the Supreme Court decision of Obergefell v. Hodges. In a 5–4 decision, the court ruled that same-sex marriage is a constitutionally guaranteed right, nullifying all state laws that bar gay and lesbian unions.

This decision institutionalized what God calls *sin*. Rather than taking a neutral position, the court chose to take an *affirming* position—which we have already seen in Romans 1:32 as the culmination of a complete rejection of God.

And yet, the path will continue to spiral downward from here. The goal of many activists is not to gain the legality of gay marriage, but to force the approval of it. Anyone who speaks out for the truth of the Word of God will be subject to threats, isolation, lawsuits, fines, and possibly jail.

In the Overgefell v. Hodges decision, the court took upon itself the right and responsibility to define marriage—a sacred institution which was already clearly defined by God. This assumed responsibility of the state hearkens back to an incident in Israel's history.

To set the context for this story, King Solomon had turned away from following God with his whole heart. As a result, God had divided the nation, selecting a man named Jeroboam to lead the new kingdom which included the ten northern tribes. God promised Jeroboam that if he would follow Him, the Lord would establish his kingdom (1 Kings 11:38). But Jeroboam was worried about losing political influence. So he forced his way into the sacred worship of God.

God's law required the people to go to Jerusalem (which was located in the southern kingdom) for the feasts to worship at the temple. Jeroboam feared that if his people went to Jerusalem three times a year, they would lose their allegiance to him and return to the leadership of Solomon's son Rehoboam. Thus, to gain approval and acceptance, Jeroboam made two golden calves, much like the one Aaron had made when the Israelites first left Egypt. He set up one in the north and one in the south of his kingdom and told the people it would be more convenient for them to worship those rather than going to Jerusalem.

And Jeroboam said in his heart, Now shall the kingdom return to the house of David: If this people go up to do sacrifice in the house of the LORD at Jerusalem, then shall the heart of this people turn again unto their lord, even unto Rehoboam king of Judah, and they shall kill me, and go again to Rehoboam king of Judah. Whereupon the king took counsel, and made two calves of gold, and said unto them, It is too much for you to go up to Jerusalem: behold thy gods, O Israel, which brought thee up out of the land of Egypt. And he set the one in Bethel, and the other put he in Dan. And this thing became a sin: for the people went to worship before the one, even unto Dan. And he made an house of high places, and made priests of

> *the lowest of the people, which were not of the*
> *sons of Levi. And Jeroboam ordained a feast in*
> *the eighth month, on the fifteenth day of the*
> *month, like unto the feast that is in Judah, and*
> *he offered upon the altar. So did he in Bethel,*
> *sacrificing unto the calves that he had made:*
> *and he placed in Bethel the priests of the high*
> *places which he had made.*—1 KINGS 12:26–32

Jeroboam's foolish act of disobedience and encroachment on God's divinely-set standard for the sake of political expedience and approval angered God. He sent a prophet to pronounce judgment on Jeroboam:

> *And, behold, there came a man of God out of*
> *Judah by the word of the LORD unto Bethel:*
> *and Jeroboam stood by the altar to burn*
> *incense. And he cried against the altar in the*
> *word of the LORD, and said, O altar, altar,*
> *thus saith the LORD; Behold, a child shall be*
> *born unto the house of David, Josiah by name;*
> *and upon thee shall he offer the priests of the*

high places that burn incense upon thee, and men's bones shall be burnt upon thee. And he gave a sign the same day, saying, This is the sign which the LORD hath spoken; Behold, the altar shall be rent, and the ashes that are upon it shall be poured out. And it came to pass, when king Jeroboam heard the saying of the man of God, which had cried against the altar in Bethel, that he put forth his hand from the altar, saying, Lay hold on him. And his hand, which he put forth against him, dried up, so that he could not pull it in again to him. The altar also was rent, and the ashes poured out from the altar, according to the sign which the man of God had given by the word of the LORD.—1 KINGS 13:1–5*

When a nation turns its back to God and rejects His right to set moral boundaries, there must be faithful Christians who will courageously proclaim the truth—even if it makes them unpopular and places their freedom and their lives at risk.

We do not know who this prophet from Judah was. His name is never given in Scripture. But we do know that he was faithful to deliver the message to a ruler who did not want to hear it.

I long and pray for national revival today. But it won't happen if we aren't willing to stand for truth.

CHAPTER 3

The Results of Rejecting

There are many Christians who, although they personally reject homosexuality, wonder if the Obergefell v. Hodges Supreme Court ruling is really that big of a deal. In the end, people are going to make their personal choices anyway, and what does it matter if the state (which has made no pretense of following Scripture for some years) disallows or sanctions those choices?

As I write, the results of this decision are just beginning to unfold. Each of the four results I'll mention here are already taking place. But I believe that some years down the road, we'll see them even more clearly and widespread.

In the words of Winston Churchill, although in an entirely different context, "This is not the end. It is not even the beginning of the end. But it is, perhaps, the end of the beginning."[29]

In what way is the legalization of same-sex marriage the end of the beginning?

The Diminishing of the Biblical Home

Our children and grandchildren will grow up in a society where same-sex marriage will be a dominant visual image. On television, in advertising, in public displays, and in countless other ways, homosexuality will constantly be in their faces, portrayed as normal and right. It will dominate the entertainment and media cultures, and anyone who opposes it will visibly be branded as a hateful bigot.

Ephesians 5:31 sets forth God's plan: "For this cause shall a man leave his father and mother, and shall be joined unto his wife, and they two shall be one flesh." God's design is for one man to marry one woman in a lifetime commitment.

The church I pastor has many vibrant families led by a single parent—a testimony to the grace of God and dedicated single parents. But even these parents would tell you that they want something different for their children and are instructing their children that, when it comes to intimacy and procreation, God has one plan.

All around us, voices cry out against the "narrow views" set forth in Scripture. People claim there cannot be just one way to Heaven and that all religions are the same. You've seen the popular bumper sticker that spells out "Coexist" with the symbols of several different religions. This is but one of many faces to the erroneous message that Jesus is one of many truths. It diminishes, indeed it contradicts, His claim that He is the only way to God: "Jesus saith unto him, I am the way, the truth, and the life: no man cometh unto the Father, but by me" (John 14:6).

Those who have attempted to diminish Christ are now diminishing the home He created. They are quite willing for a Christian to choose to marry the opposite sex as long as that Christian doesn't claim that same-sex marriage is morally wrong.

While we do our best to love our neighbors and respect those with different views, we do believe that biblical marriage is not one of many kinds of marriage, but that it is, in fact, the *only* definition of marriage.

The family was the first human institution that God created and ordained. It came before government and before the church. It is the basic building block of society. We need to be even more diligent about protecting our families and transferring biblical values to our children so they will be equipped to stand for truth—even when that means they must stand alone.

The Marginalization of Bible Believers

If you are a Christian who believes the Bible, you are not a majority in America today. And as the new minority, discrimination toward Christians will rise.

We are already seeing that those who have cried out for "tolerance" are becoming increasingly less tolerant.

If we commit to remaining faithful to the truth, there will be a price. Paul wrote, "Yea, and all that will live godly in Christ Jesus shall suffer persecution" (2 Timothy 3:12). When Paul wrote those words under the inspiration of the Holy Spirit, he was in a jail cell in Rome, from which he would soon be taken to be executed. He didn't speak of "persecution" in a theoretical sense. He had counted the cost and knew what it meant to stand for Christ.

Peter, also, endured persecution, and he wrote to suffering believers, "Beloved, think it not strange concerning the fiery trial which is to try you, as though some strange thing happened unto you: But rejoice, inasmuch as ye are partakers of Christ's sufferings; that, when his glory shall be revealed, ye may be glad also with exceeding joy. If ye be reproached for the name of Christ, happy are ye; for the spirit of glory and of God resteth upon you: on their part he is evil spoken of, but on your part he is glorified. But let none of you suffer as a murderer, or as a thief, or as an evildoer, or as a busybody in other men's matters. Yet if any man suffer as a Christian, let him not be ashamed; but let him glorify God on this behalf" (1 Peter 4:12–16).

Nowhere in Scripture are we given a promise of religious freedom, nor are we told that we will be able to exercise our faith without consequences. Standing for the truth in a society committed to lies will carry a price.

Consider, for example, Linda Barnette who worked for Grenada County, Mississippi, for twenty-four years issuing marriage licenses. Days after the Obergefell v. Hodges decision, she resigned. In her resignation letter, she wrote, "I choose to obey God rather than man. I am a follower of Christ and I believe strongly that the Bible is my final authority. The Bible teaches that a marriage is to be between a man and a woman. Therefore, because of the recent ruling of the U.S. Supreme Court, I can no longer fulfill my duties as Circuit Clerk and issue marriage licenses to same sex couples."[30]

The day when standing for God's definition of marriage may cost a person a job is not coming—it is already here. It will take time for persecution to spread (and I believe the first wave, which is just now beginning, will be primarily financial persecution), but those who love freedom and true religious liberty can see it beginning to unfold.

Quoting again from the dissent of Chief Justice John Roberts: "The majority graciously suggests that religious believers may continue to 'advocate' and 'teach' their views of marriage. The First Amendment guarantees, however, the freedom to 'exercise' religion. Ominously, that is not a word the majority use. Hard questions arise when people of faith exercise religion in ways that may be seen to conflict with the new right to same-sex marriage—when, for example, a religious college provides married student housing only to opposite-sex married couples, or a religious adoption agency declines to place children with same-sex married couples....Unfortunately, people of faith can take no comfort in the treatment they receive from the majority today."[31]

Writing separately Justice Samuel Alito declared: "I assume that those who cling to old beliefs will be able to whisper their thoughts in the recesses of their homes, but if they repeat those views in public, they will risk being labeled as bigots and treated as such by governments, employers, and schools....By imposing its own views on the entire country, the majority facilitates the marginalization of the many Americans who have traditional ideas. Recalling the harsh treatment of gays and lesbians in the past, some may think that turnabout is fair play. But if that sentiment prevails, the nation will experience bitter and lasting wounds."[32]

What we must have are Christians, churches, and families who are willing to be lights in the darkness. Peter wrote, "But ye are a chosen generation, a royal priesthood, an holy nation, a peculiar people; that ye should shew forth the praises of him who hath called you out of darkness into his marvellous light" (1 Peter 2:9).

In days past, Christians in America were simply identified as believers. Today, they are being called bigots. Tomorrow, they may be called criminals. But we should follow biblical truth anyway. Now, more than ever, we need the tenacity of the first-century church to be willing to suffer and, if need be, even die for the truth.

The Threats against Christian Education

As a pastor, I understand the Great Commission Christ gave to the church to include not just leading people to Christ, but discipling and training them in their faith. And I believe that one vital way this responsibility can be carried out is by training the next generation through Christian education. Thus, for over twenty-five years, our church has operated a Christian school as a church ministry. For the past twenty years, we've also operated a Bible college for the purpose of training students in church ministry.

Secular humanism, however, has long been the enemy of Christian education. Secular humanism is at the root of the current trends in America. It is implacably opposed to the truth of Scripture, and secular humanists have long been vocal in their disdain for Christian education. Christian schools, colleges, and universities are squarely in their crosshairs today.

During the oral arguments for Obergfell v. Hodge, Justice Alito asked the government's lawyer, Solicitor General Donald Verrilli, Jr., if colleges or universities that opposed same-sex marriage would face the possibility of losing their tax exempt status. Verilli replied, "It's certainly going to be an issue. I don't deny that."[33]

Michael Farris, Chancellor of Patrick Henry College, pointed out that it's not just institutions of higher learning that will face this threat: "No one should think that IRS implications will stop with colleges. Religious high schools, grade schools, and any other religious institution will face the same outcome. And this includes churches."[34] Indeed there have already been calls for churches to lose their tax exempt status as well.[35]

In addition to the threat of losing tax exempt status is the threat of the removal of accreditation for schools that do not fall in line and accept same sex marriage. Already at least one Christian college, Gordon College, was asked to clarify its position, although the accreditation body says the school is not at risk of losing its standing as an accredited institution.[36] Benjamin Merkle, president of New Saint Andrews College in Idaho expressed his concern that the ruling could affect Christian accreditation agencies as well, such as the Transnational Association of Christian Colleges and Schools (the body that accredits his institution).[37]

Some nominally Christian universities such as Baylor University in Waco, Texas, have already caved on the issue, changing their student conduct policy to remove the prohibition on homosexual acts.[38] Hope College in Holland, Michigan, has agreed to begin providing benefits to same sex couples.[39]

While some are dipping their sails, I believe that most biblicists will move forward in Christian education with or without tax exemption or accreditation, but these are ways the government may try to force the issue.

The Positioning of America for Judgment

It grieves me to see my country positioning herself for the judgment of God. We are today doing the very thing that Isaiah preached against hundreds of years ago—calling evil good and good evil. Isaiah warned Israel that judgment would follow: "Woe unto them that call evil good, and good evil; that put darkness for light, and light for darkness; that put bitter for sweet, and sweet for bitter!" (Isaiah 5:20). Our society can refuse to call things by their proper names. We can declare that we will approve what God has condemned. But we cannot avoid the consequences.

Chief Justice Roberts wrote, "The majority's decision is an act of will, not legal judgment....The Court invalidates the marriage laws of more than half the States and orders the transformation of a social institution that has formed the basis of human society for millennia....Just who do we think we are?"[40]

It is not new for a nation to shake its fist in God's face. Ever since men tried to build a tower to reach the heavens at Babel, people have been trying to avoid God's plan and walk their own path. It has never worked yet, and America is not going to be an exception to the common fate of nations that turn away from God. It was true when David wrote it, and it is still true today: "The wicked shall be turned into hell, and all the nations that forget God" (Psalm 9:17).

I concur with what one Christian leader wrote on his Facebook page, "I pray God will spare America from His judgment, though, by our actions as a nation, we give Him less and less reason to do so."[41]

Even Thomas Jefferson recognized the impossibility of maintaining religious freedoms while denying their source: "And can the liberties of a nation be thought secure when we have removed their only firm basis, a conviction in the minds of the people that these liberties are the gift of God? That they are not to be violated but with his wrath? Indeed I tremble for my country when I reflect that God is just: that his justice cannot sleep forever." His words are largely ignored in Washington today, although they are carved into the stone wall of the Jefferson Memorial.

And Yet...

Although every result mentioned in this chapter—the diminishing of the biblical home, marginalization of Bible believers, threats against Christian education, and positioning of America for the judgment of God—is real and serious, there are plenty of reasons to be encouraged.

God is certainly not finished with Christianity in America. Perhaps we will be called upon as never before to stand for truth, but this day of "Laodicean," or lukewarm, Christianity may have needed such a wake up call—the kind that will raise up men and women of God to pave the way for future generations to have freedom and know Christ.

Consider a few truths from the Word of God and from history:

The gospel is more powerful than any government. When Communism arose in brutal fashion in China, there were perhaps three million Christians in the entire country. Today, even with heavy persecution against Christians, conservative estimates say there are well over 200 million Christians in that country. You simply cannot shackle the gospel of Christ.

Remember that it was from prison with guards on either side of him that Paul wrote, "For I am not ashamed of the gospel of Christ: for it is the power of God unto salvation to every one that believeth; to the Jew first, and also to the Greek" (Romans 1:16). Yes! The gospel is the power of God, and, as such, it is more powerful than human verdicts.

We often see great spiritual progress after dark spiritual times. I enjoy studying Baptist history and am also inspired by the faith of the Reformers. I have visited the cave churches of the Waldensians of the twelfth century and the site of the burning of Huss, Latimer, Ridley, and others. We celebrate the faith and courage of those who gave their lives for the faith, and we are aware that millions trusted Christ because a few were willing to stand.

We should never forget that just before the Reformation or the Great Awakening or even the rise of soulwinning Baptist churches in the '70s and '80s, there were periods known as the "Dark Ages" or the "sexual revolution." These were times when many were hopeless, but the Word of God was not bound.

We often see the greatest spiritual progress in the darkest of times. When things are going well, we don't sense a need for God's power and a moving of the Holy Spirit. But when the darkness spreads, we long for the light. God does not mean for us to be defeated. He calls us to take a stand, confident in the knowledge that He is in control.

Jesus said, "These things I have spoken unto you, that in me ye might have peace. In the world ye shall have tribulation: but be of good cheer; I have overcome the world" (John 16:33). And 1 John 5:4 confirms, "For whatsoever is born of God overcometh the world: and this is the victory that overcometh the world, even our faith."

Christ is still building His church. I will never forget my friend and mentor Dr. Curtis Hutson singing at a pastors' meeting in North Carolina around 1995. His body was filled with cancer, and his days were drawing to an end. The song he chose? It was entitled, "I'm on the Winning Side." While he may not have appeared so to those who didn't know Christ, Dr. Hutson was on the winning side, and so are those of us who are in Christ.

Jesus declared His intention to keep building His church until the end of the age: "And I say also unto thee, That thou art Peter, and upon this rock I will build my church; and the gates of hell shall not prevail against it" (Matthew 16:18). We are not alone in this fight. The Lord who loves us and saved us is leading us. He is not just the kind and gentle Shepherd—He is also the Captain of the hosts of Heaven, and no power on Earth can stand against Him.

What do these truths mean for us today? In short, they mean we live out our faith as never before, confident in the power of the gospel to change lives. They mean that we must live in and respond to the culture around us as Bible-believing Christians who are filled with the Spirit and courageous in our witness. Let's look at the specifics of our response in Part 2.

PART TWO

The Response of the Biblical Minority

Two hundred and twelve years after Jeroboam led the northern nation of Israel into idolatry, the country was conquered by the Assyrians. The royal family and the middle class were taken captive, but the poor and down-and-outers were left behind—destitute and desolate.

About one hundred years later, King Josiah came along. God had kindled in his heart a desire to seek the Lord and to lead the southern nation of Judah back to the worship of God. As Josiah moved through the land cleaning up the idols and their altars, he came to Jeroboam's altar in Bethel. Here he fulfilled the prophecy against it as well as honored the prophet who had so boldly spoken it:

> *Moreover the altar that was at Bethel, and the high place which Jeroboam the son of Nebat, who made Israel to sin, had made, both that altar and the high place he brake down, and burned the high place, and stamped it small to powder, and burned the grove. And as Josiah turned himself, he spied the sepulchres that were*

there in the mount, and sent, and took the bones
out of the sepulchres, and burned them upon
the altar, and polluted it, according to the word
of the LORD *which the man of God proclaimed,*
who proclaimed these words. Then he said,
What title is that that I see? And the men of the
city told him, It is the sepulchre of the man of
God, which came from Judah, and proclaimed
these things that thou hast done against the
altar of Bethel. And he said, Let him alone; let
no man move his bones. So they let his bones
alone, with the bones of the prophet that came
out of Samaria.—2 KINGS 23:15–18

But Josiah didn't stop there. He reinstituted the
passover (one of the feasts which Jeroboam had feared
and replaced with false worship), not just for Judah,
but for all Israelites willing to come and partake. And
as it happened, descendents of those tribes which
Jeroboam had led into idolatry joined with Judah in
the revival of worshipping God.

And there was no passover like to that kept in Israel from the days of Samuel the prophet; neither did all the kings of Israel keep such a passover as Josiah kept, and the priests, and the Levites, and all Judah and Israel that were present, and the inhabitants of Jerusalem.—2 CHRONICLES 35:18

After national apostasy and divine judgment, they finally turned *back to God.*

CHAPTER 4

Never Be Ashamed of the Gospel of Christ

Ralph was in serious trouble, but not doing much to help himself. "Ralph," his friend admonished, "you've got two hands. Why don't you do something?"

"I am," Ralph replied. "I'm wringing both of them!"

American Christians have a distinct tendency to worry and complain about the downward trend of our nation without doing much to affect change. But we must do more than worry. We must act in decisively God-honoring, Christ-exalting, gospel-promoting ways.

To understand what that kind of action would look like, we need look no further than the New Testament. For as we have already observed, New Testament Christians served the Lord and proclaimed the gospel of Christ in a perverse and wicked culture. How, specifically, did they do it?

In this day of biblical minority, it's time for us to have a plan of action. Christ has called us to be salt and light in our world. Will we live in discouragement and fear, hiding our light, or will we hold forth the light, letting it shine boldly against the darkness? Will we blend in, losing our savor? Or will we confidently and victoriously season our society with truth and grace?

In these next chapters, I'd like to point out eight responses that we, as the biblical minority, must take to honor the Lord and make a difference in our culture.

In the same chapter that Paul defined the godless, pagan lifestyles of the Gentile world, he said, "I am debtor both to the Greeks, and to the Barbarians; both to the wise, and to the unwise. So, as much as in me is, I am ready to preach the gospel to you that are at Rome also. For I am not ashamed of the gospel of Christ: for it is the power of God unto salvation to every one that believeth; to the Jew first, and also to the Greek" (Romans 1:14–16).

Paul recognized the sensual perverse culture that surrounded him, but he wasn't wringing his hands about it. As he looked at the various groups and subcultures around him, instead of withdrawing as a monk or a hermit, he intensified his commitment to preach the gospel. There is no human society so depraved or so wicked that it is immune to the gospel.

Understand, those around us who live in or promote ungodly, immoral lifestyles are not our enemies—they are our mission field. There must be Christians and local churches who will rise up and boldly, compassionately, and gracefully declare the single truth people steeped in sin need—the death, burial, and resurrection of Christ for our sins. They don't need a new morality or our arguments. My arguments and your arguments will never change someone's heart. They need Christ. They need the indwelling Holy Spirit—the only one who can change a heart through the new birth.

While it would be nice if the Supreme Court came back next year and reversed their foolish and ungodly decision, that would not solve our nation's biggest problem. It would be wonderful if we elected leaders who respected the Constitution and the limits on government it imposes, but that would not solve our biggest problem. In the final analysis, we do not have a government problem so much as a sin problem. Yet, it seems that we Christians have lost what this world needs.

I thank the Lord for Christians who march against abortion, write congressmen, and lobby for religious freedoms. But please make no mistake; there is one issue that must reign supreme in the heart and on the lips of every Christian—the gospel of Jesus Christ.

Paul instructed the church at Philippi, "That ye may be blameless and harmless, the sons of God, without rebuke, *in the midst of a crooked and perverse nation, among whom ye shine as lights in the world; Holding forth the word of life...*" (Philippians 2:15–16). If there has ever been a "crooked and perverse nation"—a God-forsaking nation—it is the United States of America. And that is the very reason we must hold forth the word of life. In the deepening darkness, it will shine all the more brightly.

As Christians, our greatest responsibility is not to push against the cultural trends by social or political means, although I do believe we should exercise our freedom to vote and should encourage leaders who will stand for truth. Our greatest responsibility, however, is to obey the orders of our Captain when He said, "...Go ye into all the world, and preach the gospel..." (Mark 16:15).

Rather than being discouraged, and hunkering down to ride out the storm, the most needful response is to do more than ever to reach people with the gospel. When Jesus said that the gates of Hell would not be able to prevail against the church, He was not saying that the enemy would be unable to *defeat* the church. He was declaring that the enemy would be unable to *resist* the church. We are supposed to be on the offensive. The only cure to sin problems—whether we are talking about homosexuality or any other sin— is the gospel.

CHAPTER 5

Love and Forgive Those Who Oppose God's Word

Those who have made their rally cry, "Tolerance" to get to the position of the majority do not simply want tolerance. They want dominance. And they will be—indeed, they are already becoming— totalitarians in enforcing it. Now that they have carved out homosexuality as the new normal, they won't be preaching tolerance. They won't be having anti-bullying days in public schools in support of Christian children who are discriminated against; they will *be* the bullies.

In the months preceding the decision of Obergefell v. Hodges, as the decision was being weighed and the oral arguments presented to the Supreme Court, I don't know of a period when I've had more profanity coming through my various inboxes. Call after call, email after email, public and private messages through social media streams …things said by the tolerance crowd were unrepeatable.

There is a very real temptation to want to treat them the same way they treat us, especially given some of the things that supporters of same-sex marriage are saying and doing. But that is a grave error. We will never argue, condemn, or belittle anyone into the Kingdom of God. "Jesus said unto him, Thou shalt love the Lord thy God with all thy heart, and with all thy soul, and with all thy mind. This is the first and great commandment. And the second is like unto it, Thou shalt love thy neighbour as thyself" (Matthew 22:37–39).

We must remember who our enemy is—Satan. "For we wrestle not against flesh and blood, but against principalities, against powers, against the rulers of the darkness of this world, against spiritual wickedness in high places" (Ephesians 6:12).

And we must remember what our weapons are—prayer, the gospel, and the love of God. "For the weapons of our warfare are not carnal, but mighty through God to the pulling down of strong holds" (2 Corinthians 10:4).

I believe that in coming years, there will be many people who will be disillusioned by what they thought homosexuality and same-sex marriage would give them. There will be people who discover in real and painful ways that immoral relationships could not fill the void in their souls. And when that happens, I want to be there to offer them the love of God as expressed in the gospel of Jesus Christ.

Consider the woman at the well. When Christ met her, she had already been through multiple immoral relationships, and she was experiencing that they couldn't satisfy. For some time, she had tried to fill the needs in her heart by "another relationship." But her soul was still thirsty. And Jesus—full of grace and truth—confronted her sin with the offer of salvation. He treated her with respect and kindness, and she listened to His message. That day, she not only found the Water of Life, but she also became a dynamic witness to others.

If our response as Christians is returning evil for evil, hatred for hatred, name calling for name calling, how will those who finally find themselves in need of the love of God know what they need or where to find it?

One Christian writer said it well: "The church must prepare for the refugees from the sexual revolution. There are two sorts of churches that will not be able to reach the sexual revolution's refugees. A church that has given up on the truth of the Scriptures, including on marriage and sexuality, and has nothing to say to a fallen world. And a church that screams with outrage at those who disagree will have nothing to say to those who are looking for a new birth. We must stand with conviction and with kindness, with truth and with grace."[42]

I recognize that if same-sex marriage is the new orthodoxy—and it is—all who oppose are deemed haters in this new America. But we must preach Christ's love anyway.

I am going to continue preaching against sin. If the government says we cannot say homosexuality is wrong, I am going to declare, "Thus saith the Lord." But I am going to be careful to do it in such a way that magnifies the grace of God in providing the blood of Jesus as payment for every sin, praying that those who need help will listen to the gospel rather than closing their hearts and minds to the truth.

CHAPTER 6

Hold to the Truth

Because of the wisdom of our founding fathers, Christians in the United States have enjoyed a level of religious freedom rare in human history. As that begins to change, we must stand fast against those who counsel trimming the message to become more acceptable to the world. Dr. David Gibbs, Jr., founder and president of the Christian Law Association, offered a wise perspective: "This is one of the most challenging and exciting times for Christians in the history of America. We must do the right thing, the right way. It is a privilege and an honor to stand biblically for the cause of Jesus Christ."[43]

As noted earlier, our government is becoming increasingly hostile toward the truth. What if the time comes when the government not only encroaches on religious freedom, but mandates you compromise your conscience and act against the Word of God? I believe that time is coming. Indeed, it already has come for some Americans.

It behooves us to develop a scriptural understanding of what it means to hold to the truth before that time comes for us.

We must first recognize that by and large we are to submit to man's ordinances. First Peter 2:13–14 instructs, "Submit yourselves to every ordinance of man for the Lord's sake: whether it be to the king, as supreme; Or unto governors, as unto them that are sent by him for the punishment of evildoers, and for the praise of them that do well."

Bible-believing Christians should be the best citizens of any city. We should subordinate ourselves to the civil ordinances of those in positions of authority. (As Americans, we have the added privilege of selecting our authorities through the political process. Although this freedom may yield increasingly limited influence as Bible-believing Christians become a greater minority, we should use it nonetheless.) Regardless of who is in authority, we should willingly and peacefully submit.

As Christians, we recognize that human authority was established and ordained by God. When Paul penned the following words, he couldn't have even comprehended the level of freedom we enjoy today. Yet he instructed, "Let every soul be subject unto the higher powers. For there is no power but of God: the powers that be are ordained of God. Whosoever therefore resisteth the power, resisteth the ordinance of God: and they that resist shall receive to themselves damnation" (Romans 13:1–2).

It is ridiculous and unbecoming to the gospel of Christ for Christians to become belligerent toward the standard laws of the land (such as traffic laws or building and fire codes) put in place to insure the safety of all citizens. We should submit ourselves and be a blessing to those who rule over us.

At the same time, however, we recognize that our ultimate authority is God. Where human authority directly commands us to act contrary to God's authority, we must choose to submit to God. Peter—who penned the verses above instructing us to submit to every ordinance of man—found himself in such a position. When he and the other apostles were commanded to stop preaching, they simply answered, "We ought to obey God rather than men" (Acts 5:29).

Our ultimate authority is God, and our ultimate guide is His Word. When government commands us to disobey the Bible, we must choose to obey God instead. There are a number of clear Bible examples for disobedience to man in obedience to God—examples where God honored and rewarded those who were faithful to Him.

During the captivity of the Israelites in Egypt, Pharaoh ordered the Hebrew midwives to kill all of the male babies as soon as they were born. Rather than obeying that evil edict, the Hebrew midwives saved the boys alive. They feared God more than they feared an absolute monarch who could have them killed with a single word. "Therefore God dealt well with the midwives: and the people multiplied, and waxed very mighty. And it came to pass, because the midwives feared God, that he made them houses" (Exodus 1:20–21).

When the Babylonians carried some of the best young men of Judah into captivity to train them to serve in their empire, they attempted to sever the young men's loyalty to their home and their God. Yet when Nebuchadnezzar threatened to have anyone killed who would not bow down to his golden statue, three young men refused. Even when Nebuchadnezar offered them the chance to reconsider and save their lives, they remained faithful. "Shadrach, Meshach, and Abednego, answered and said to the king, O Nebuchadnezzar, we are not careful to answer thee in this matter. If it be so, our God whom we serve is able to deliver us from the burning fiery furnace, and he will deliver us out of thine hand, O king. But if not, be it known unto thee, O king, that we will not serve thy gods, nor worship the golden image which thou hast set up" (Daniel 3:16–18).

Daniel, also taken captive from Judah as a young man, established such a sterling witness and reputation for both his faith and his integrity that his enemies knew their only chance of finding anything against him was to cast his commitment to God in a negative light. And they were right. Even after they connived a plan to make prayer to God illegal, Daniel prayed. "Now when Daniel knew that the writing was signed, he went into his house; and his windows being open in his chamber toward Jerusalem, he kneeled upon his knees three times a day, and prayed, and gave thanks before his God, as he did aforetime. Then these men assembled, and found Daniel praying and making supplication before his God" (Daniel 6:10–11).

The powerful preaching of the apostles rocked the city of Jerusalem. The Jewish leaders tried everything to get them to stop preaching. They arrested them, beat them, and sternly commanded them to stop preaching. Yet Peter and John and the others continued to declare the message that Jesus was the Messiah and the only hope of salvation. "And when they had brought them, they set them before the council: and the high priest asked them, Saying, Did not we straitly command you that ye should not teach in this name? and, behold, ye have filled Jerusalem with your doctrine, and intend to bring this man's blood upon us. Then Peter and the other apostles answered and said, We ought to obey God rather than men" (Acts 5:27–29).

Our allegiance is first and foremost to the Lord Jesus Christ. If we reach the point where it becomes necessary, I am prepared for civil disobedience. We will not marry a same sex couple at Lancaster Baptist Church. We will not allow immorality at West Coast Baptist College. We will not stop preaching and teaching that homosexuality is a sin against God's order. If the government insists we act contrary to Scripture, we cannot comply. If that means I have to go to jail, I will. I would certainly not want to do so, but I must obey God rather than man. If that means we lose our tax exempt status, we will still not change our message. I would rather lose every one of the beautiful buildings that have been constructed with the sacrificial gifts of God's people than be disloyal to the God who led us to build them. Christ purchased the church with His blood (Acts 20:28). Thus, it does not belong to the State, but to the Lord.

Remember, God does not promise physical deliverance for obedience. There are times when He intervenes to halt the consequences of obeying Him instead of man, but there are also times when He allows His people to suffer. Peter preached faithfully and saw thousands saved. Stephen preached faithfully and was stoned to death. Both held to the truth, but neither had the promise of physical deliverance.

John Quincy Adams served only a single term in office as President before being defeated for reelection by Andrew Jackson. Rather than sitting at home and sulking because he had been turned out of office, Adams ran for and won a seat in Congress, where he spent most of the rest of his life trying to end the practice of slavery. Though his results bore little fruit in his lifetime, Adams persisted in doing what was right. He often said, "Duties are ours. Results are God's."

All of us would prefer to avoid persecution and suffering. There are many Christians around the world who have never been able to meet openly in a church or share their faith, yet they have remained faithful. Our commitment to the truth needs to be so strong that if the time comes when we are forced to choose between obeying God and obeying man, we will serve Him, no matter what happens as a result.

CHAPTER 7

Teach Your Children

The hardest-hit targets of the campaign for same-sex marriage are young people. There is a carefully-crafted agenda that has been underway for decades to indoctrinate and recruit young people to ungodly lifestyles and to convince them that God's ways are harsh, judgmental, and inapplicable to the age in which we live. Adolf Hitler, in a speech shortly before he assumed full power over Germany, said, "When an opponent declares, 'I will not come over to your side,' I calmly say, 'Your child belongs to us already.... What are you? You will pass on. Your descendants, however, now stand in the new camp. In a short time they will know nothing else but this new community.'"[44] This is a similar mentality with which LGBT activists work to gain acceptance and approval for their cause in the hearts and minds of young people.

It has always been critical for Christian parents to instill the Word of God into the hearts of their children, but now it is more vital than ever before. This is God's plan for protecting a child and shaping the future of a nation. "And these words, which I command thee this day, shall be in thine heart: And thou shalt teach them diligently unto thy children, and shalt talk of them when thou sittest in thine house, and when thou walkest by the way, and when thou liest down, and when thou risest up. And thou shalt bind them for a sign upon thine hand, and they shall be as frontlets between thine eyes. And thou shalt write them upon the posts of thy house, and on thy gates" (Deuteronomy 6:6–9).

For many years now our culture has been saturated with messages that devalue Christian teaching and hold up ungodliness as valid alternatives. The media—movies, television, music, theater, and comic books—have openly and unapologetically promoted homosexuality. Even in the public schools, the so called "anti-bullying program" is often just a promotion of the gay agenda. (For the record, I'm against bullying any child for any reason. I've just seen that there is more to the anti-bullying programs than anti-bullying.) Many Christian parents have been undiscerning of what is being taught and have allowed this propaganda to fill the minds of their children.

Wise parents need to be on guard, setting boundaries for what they will allow their children to see, hear, sing, and share with others. They need to know who their children's friends are, what they are being taught in school, and what is influencing them. There needs to be careful filtering in place so that things do not slip through the cracks of the defenses you have set up around your home.

What's more, Christian parents need to model the biblical design for the family to their children. Young people need to see their dad treat his wife with deference, love, care, and respect. They need to see a healthy marriage relationship and observe that love is not all about having a partner that brings sensual satisfaction but about fulfillment in a commitment to a spouse and obedience to God. If you are a single parent, remember that one of the blessings of being part of a church family is that your children will have opportunity to see these examples in other Christian families in the church. Be faithful in attendance, and point your child to godly role models.

Above everything else, our job as parents is to saturate our children's hearts and minds with Scripture. The only way that they can stand against the lies of the culture is if they know the truth of Christ— not what their parents know or believe, but what they have internalized for themselves. Our children and grandchildren will not grow up in the same kind of society in which we grew up. They must be prepared before they leave our homes to face the challenges that their faith will have to endure.

The good news is that this is possible! Yes, our young people are targeted with an ungodly agenda.

But, as parents and grandparents, God has given us powerful influence into their hearts—if we will seize it.

Consider Timothy, whose Greek father was apparently an unbeliever. Yet even growing up in the ungodly, sensual Greek culture, Timothy's mother and grandmother so instilled God's Word and biblical truth into his heart that he held fast to the faith. In 2 Timothy, the Apostle Paul made two references to the early training in Timothy's life by his mother and grandmother: "When I call to remembrance the unfeigned faith that is in thee, which dwelt first in thy grandmother Lois, and thy mother Eunice; and I am persuaded that in thee also....And that from a child thou hast known the holy scriptures, which are able to make thee wise unto salvation through faith which is in Christ Jesus" (2 Timothy 1:5, 3:15).

In the Old Testament, we see Moses, who only had a short time—a few years at most—with his mother (Exodus 2:7–10). Yet, when he came of age, the values and his identity as one of God's people which Jocabed had instilled into his young heart guided his choices: "By faith Moses, when he was come to years, refused to be called the son of Pharaoh's daughter; Choosing rather to suffer affliction with the people of God, than to enjoy the pleasures of sin for a season" (Hebrews 11:24–25).

Then there was the Israelite girl who was captured by the Syrians and taken to serve as a slave in the house of the Syrian general Naaman. This young girl who had been ripped from her home and godly influences had such a deep faith and commitment to God instilled in her heart that when she learned that Naaman had leprosy, she told his wife that the prophet Elisha would be able to heal him. Her faith is particularly amazing when you consider that Elisha had never healed a leper before. (See Luke 4:27.) She had been brought up to believe that God's power working through God's man could accomplish the impossible.

As Christian parents, we cannot abdicate our responsibility to invest in our children's lives and to teach them the Word of God. Protect your children, pray for their salvation, encourage their growth in the Lord, and instill God's truth into their souls.

CHAPTER 8

Assemble with Believers

The more pressure we are under from the outside world, the more we need the strength and encouragement that comes from the fellowship of the local church. Hebrews 10:23–25 connects holding to the truth and assembling with other Christians, and it admonishes us to do both: "Let us hold fast the profession of our faith without wavering; (for he is faithful that promised;) And let us consider one another to provoke unto love and to good works: Not forsaking the assembling of ourselves together, as the manner of some is; but exhorting one another: and so much the more, as ye see the day approaching."

If I were not the pastor of Lancaster Baptist Church, I would still be there every time the doors were open. I need the fellowship, encouragement, prayers, singing, teaching, and preaching for my own life and spiritual health, not just for the sake of the church.

There will be difficult days ahead for Christians as our culture continues throwing off moral restraints and opposing all who object. Discouragement will abound, and weak Christians—disconnected from the body of Christ—won't survive. They will cave and blend in with the culture or become despondent and defeated. Like the first-century churches, we will need to assemble and support one another—to encourage each other and to strengthen one another.

If you have seen the giant redwood trees we have here in California, I'm sure you've been amazed by how big they are. They tower hundreds of feet into the air. Yet for their great size, they actually have shallow roots that only go a few feet underground. Rather than going deep, they stretch out horizontally. The roots of the trees interweave with each other, and the giant redwoods last because they hold each other up when the storms come. That is the reason church is so important. In the days ahead, we are going to need each other more than ever before.

CHAPTER 9

Encourage Bible-Based Political Leaders

One of the ramifications of the new majority's intolerance will be the need for new laws protecting religious freedom and the expression of religion guaranteed in our Constitution. Thankfully, we do have leaders serving as elected officials who are committed to vote for our freedom. We need to encourage these leaders—pray for them, write them, thank them, and exercise our right to vote for them.

Paul never had the opportunity to elect government officials as we do here in the United

States, but he was very willing to use his rights as a Roman citizen. On one occasion he used these rights to have false accusations publicly expunged: "But Paul said unto them, They have beaten us openly uncondemned, being Romans, and have cast us into prison; and now do they thrust us out privily? nay verily; but let them come themselves and fetch us out. And the serjeants told these words unto the magistrates: and they feared, when they heard that they were Romans" (Acts 16:37–38). On another occasion, he used his citizenship to avoid a beating: "And as they bound him with thongs, Paul said unto the centurion that stood by, Is it lawful for you to scourge a man that is a Roman, and uncondemned? When the centurion heard that, he went and told the chief captain, saying, Take heed what thou doest: for this man is a Roman" (Acts 22:25–26).

In the coming days, discrimination toward Christians in the public sector will become more common. Men and women will be treated as second-class citizens simply because they are Christians. We should encourage efforts to protect churches, Christian schools, Christian business owners, and Christians across every sector of society from being forced to go against their faith or hide what they believe. Brian S. Brown of the National Organization for Marriage said, "We call on Congress and state governments to move immediately to protect the rights of people who believe in the truth of marriage from being discriminated against by passing the First Amendment Defense Act through Congress, and similar legislation in the various states."[45]

Incidentally, freedom to exercise religion is one of the Bible-based founding principles of our country. It is from Scripture that we derive the belief that man has a free will and should not be forced to violate his God-given conscience.

America's problem is not primarily a political problem—it is a spiritual problem. The only real and lasting solution is the gospel. At the same time, having godly leaders helps set the stage for improving the current situation, as well as protecting the rights we are supposed to have.

CHAPTER 10

Pray for Revival in Our Nation

As dark as the future looks, I don't believe our situation is hopeless. God has worked in the past in great and mighty ways, shaking entire cities and nations with His power and turning many to repentance. There has never been a revival anywhere in human history that was not preceded by a turning away from God—for without that, there is no need for revival. There is hope for any nation—not from changed political policies or better social reforms, but through a turning to God. We don't look to the government or society at large for change; we ask God to revive His church.

Remember that God told Abraham He would spare Sodom if there were ten righteous people found there. The problem was that Lot had not been faithful and there were not even ten believers. We can work and pray and witness and do our part to ensure that there are righteous people in our city. We can yield ourselves to God and fervently pray for nation-wide revival.

Revival does not start "out there"—it starts within the church. If churches across America were shaken with a fervor and intense desire to see God work, our culture would soon be impacted. Our nation may not turn back to God as a whole, but if we do not turn from our current path, we will surely suffer His judgment. As bad as the situation seems to be today, there is still a solution available. God made a wonderful promise to Solomon at the dedication of the temple. Though it was primarily intended for the people of Israel, the principle is applicable to us today. "If my people, which are called by my name, shall humble themselves, and pray, and seek my face, and turn from their wicked ways; then will I hear from heaven, and will forgive their sin, and will heal their land" (2 Chronicles 7:14).

As my friend Dr. R. B. Ouellette said, "To say that America is beyond hope is to deny the possibility of revival and to doubt the power of God." I believe that God is fully in control, but that He also calls us to be fully engaged—in prayer. "…The effectual fervent prayer of a righteous man availeth much" (James 5:16).

CHAPTER 11

Live in the Hope
of Christ's Return

Finally, we need to live in the hope of the Lord's return. The foundations of society may shift and crumble, but the foundations of our faith remain secure. We have been given the promise that the Lord will return, and this promise is a source of comfort and encouragement to us during difficult days. "For the Lord himself shall descend from heaven with a shout, with the voice of the archangel, and with the trump of God: and the dead in Christ shall rise first: Then we which are alive and remain shall be caught up together with them in the clouds, to meet the Lord in the air: and so shall we ever be with the Lord. Wherefore comfort one another with these words" (1 Thessalonians 4:16–18).

In addition to being a source of hope and comfort, the certainty of the Lord's return should change the way that we live. The Apostle John, in 1 John 3:1–3 marvels at the love of God and points out that because of it, we are different from the world and should be living holy lives in anticipation of Christ's return: "Behold, what manner of love the Father hath bestowed upon us, that we should be called the sons of God: therefore the world knoweth us not, because it knew him not. Beloved, now are we the sons of God, and it doth not yet appear what we shall be: but we know that, when he shall appear, we shall be like him; for we shall see him as he is. And every man that hath this hope in him purifieth himself, even as he is pure."

The world loves to mock the moral failures of Christians. They point to the failed marriages of believers as a form of proof that we don't value marriage as we say we do...and they have a point. The grace of God not only gives us salvation, but it teaches us to live godly, holy lives with the anticipation of Christ's return. "For the grace of God that bringeth salvation hath appeared to all men, Teaching us that, denying ungodliness and worldly lusts, we should live soberly, righteously, and godly, in this present world; Looking for that blessed hope, and the glorious appearing of the great God and our Saviour Jesus Christ" (Titus 2:11–13).

Keeping our focus on the return of Jesus will help ensure that we live righteously and will not give unbelievers reason to reject the gospel. The qualifications that Paul wrote to Timothy for pastors apply to all of us in this regard: "Moreover he must have a good report of them which are without; lest he fall into reproach and the snare of the devil" (1 Timothy 3:7). Let us be witnesses above reproach as we await the coming of the Lord.

CONCLUSION

Loyal to Christ

When the New Testament was written to the early church, Christians were a tiny minority. The Jewish leaders hated them, going so far as to send people out to persecute and oppose Christians wherever they could find them. The Romans were not impressed with this new religion either. They were willing for people to worship pretty much anything as long as they were willing to also acknowledge the divinity of the emperor. But Christians insisted that there was only one God, and this made them unpopular with—and targeted by—the government.

Against this background, Peter wrote to the suffering and persecuted believers scattered across the Roman Empire. Meditate for a moment on these words:

Blessed be the God and Father of our Lord Jesus Christ, which according to his abundant mercy hath begotten us again unto a lively hope by the resurrection of Jesus Christ from the dead, To an inheritance incorruptible, and undefiled, and that fadeth not away, reserved in heaven for you, Who are kept by the power of God through faith unto salvation ready to be revealed in the last time. Wherein ye greatly rejoice, though now for a season, if need be, ye are in heaviness through manifold temptations: That the trial of your faith, being much more precious than of gold that perisheth, though it be tried with fire, might be found unto praise and honour and glory at the appearing of Jesus Christ: Whom having not seen, ye love; in whom, though now ye

see him not, yet believing, ye rejoice with joy
unspeakable and full of glory: Receiving the
end of your faith, even the salvation of your
souls.—1 PETER 1:3–9

When we take a stand for the faith and are loyal to Jesus Christ, even if it means opposing the culture, we are following in the footsteps of godly men and women who have been faithful, even unto death. We possess a long heritage of those who have been loyal to Christ, and their testimonies spur us forward in standing for Jesus.

Here are brief historical sketches of just five Christians who loved their Lord more than their lives:

Peter Waldo (1140–1217)

Peter Waldo was a wealthy merchant when he took a vow of poverty in hopes of obtaining salvation. With time on his hands and hunger in his heart, he began studying Scripture and found the true way of salvation—through the blood of Jesus Christ.

Waldo begin sharing the gospel with others. He led so many to Christ—and taught them to be soulwinners as well—that critics complained his followers were *everywhere* preaching the gospel. Eventually, the Catholic priests demanded he and his followers be silenced, labeled Waldo as a heretic, and banished him from the city of Lyons, France.

Waldo and his followers (who came to be called Waldensians) went to the Piedmont Valley on the border of France and Italy. There, living and teaching in caves in the hills, Waldo kept preaching and training others until he died in 1217.

Centuries later, in 1655, thousands of Waldensians—still preaching the gospel—were brutally killed in the historic "Massacre in Piedmont" because they would not recant their faith.

John Huss (1369–1415)

Born in Bohemia (modern day Czech Republic), John Huss was raised in the church of Rome and became a Roman Catholic priest. Through studying Scripture,

Huss came to salvation and began to preach salvation by grace. He was excommunicated and called before a council in Constance, Germany, to stand trial. At the trial Huss testified to salvation through grace alone and was sentenced to die at the stake.

When Huss was being chained to the stake at which he would be burned alive, he said, "My Lord Jesus Christ was bound with a harder 'chain' than this for my sake, and why then should I be ashamed of this rusty one?" Just before the fire was lit, the imperial marshall urged Huss to recant. He replied, "No, what I taught with my lips I seal with my blood." Surrounded by flames, Huss sang, "Christ, thou Son of the living God, have mercy upon me" until he entered the presence of the Lord.

Hugh Latimer (1487–1555)

Latimer studied at Cambridge, England, eventually becoming the Cambridge chaplain. It was through the testimony of preachers who were later burned for heresy that Latimer was saved. As Latimer himself began to preach the truth of the gospel, he too was imprisoned. As political winds changed, he was eventually released.

After Queen Mary I (known in history as "Bloody Mary") took the throne, however, Latimer was once again arrested and imprisoned. At his formal sentencing—to be burned at the stake—Latimer (nearly seventy years old by now) said, "I thank God most heartily that He hath prolonged my life to this end, that I may in this case glorify God by that kind of death."

I've stood at the very wall where the flames leapt up around Latimer and Nicholas Ridley (who was burned with him for also taking a stand for Christ). Even as the fire raged around their bodies, Latimer said to Ridley, "Play the man, Master Ridley; we shall this day light such a candle, by God's grace, in England, as I trust shall never be put out."

John Bunyan (1628-1688)

John Bunyan, of Bedford, England, lived a godless, wicked life as a young man. But in 1653, he was saved under the ministry of a nonconformist preacher (a preacher who was not under the authority of the Church of England, the state church at the time). Within a few years, Bunyan himself was preaching as an itinerant nonconformist preacher in surrounding villages and towns.

In 1660, as he was preaching, Bunyan was arrested for preaching without the license of the Church of England. (Obtaining such a license was not simply a matter of registering with the state, in the way that churches today register for a tax-exempt status. Rather, it was the way in which the state—through the "state church"—could refuse men the right to preach by withholding a license and could censor the preaching of those to whom they did grant a license.)

Originally, Bunyan was sentenced to three months in prison, with his release hinging on whether or not he would promise to give up preaching. He wouldn't, and he spent twelve years in prison as a result. From prison, Bunyan made thread laces to try to support his wife and four children (including a blind daughter). He also wrote his famed allegory of the Christian life, *Pilgrim's Progress*.

Obadiah Holmes (1610–1682)

After he was saved in 1638, Obadiah Holmes and his wife sailed to the young colony of Massachusetts. It was there that Holmes became convinced from Scripture of the autonomy of the local church and that infant baptism was unscriptural. He was then baptized and became a Baptist preacher himself.

The religious and political climate in the early American colonies was similar to that of England; there was a state church (in Massachusetts, it was the Congregational Church) and there was little religious freedom to those outside of it. For that reason, Holmes moved to Rhode Island (the first of the American Colonies to grant true religious liberty for people of any denomination or religion). But in 1651, Holmes was arrested while holding a preaching service in Massachusetts. He was publicly flogged—thirty lashes with a three-chord whip. The beating was so severe that for weeks he could only lie on his stomach or be propped up on his hands and knees.

Holmes later became the pastor of the Baptist church in Newport, where he served for thirty years until his death. His story was often referenced in later years by Baptists who paved the way for religious freedom in America.

Victory in Jesus

When I think of these and so many more men and women who stood for Christ in the midst of tremendous opposition and persecution, I'm reminded of two truths: First, I don't want to be the weak link in the chain for my generation. And second, the grace of God is sufficient for any suffering we encounter as a result of loyalty to Christ.

What kept these men going in the face of persecution and even death? How did they stand strong when few others were willing to pay the price? They understood that ultimately they were following

Christ who gives us victory. This is what you and I must hold in our hearts in these days of challenge.

The Apostle Peter, no stranger to persecution, challenged persecuted believers, "Wherefore gird up the loins of your mind, be sober, and hope to the end for the grace that is to be brought unto you at the revelation of Jesus Christ" (1 Peter 1:13).

May we as God's people take our place in standing for our Lord Jesus Christ. May we follow the biblical admonitions outlined in this book to declare the gospel, love the lost, and live in light of eternity.

Regardless of where our culture goes or the difficulties that we as the Christian minority face in the days ahead, I challenge you: Know what you believe. Know who you follow. And be assured that, no matter how things may appear, Christ is still building His church.

> *...upon this rock I will build my church; and the gates of hell shall not prevail against it.*
> —Matthew 16:18

Introduction

1   Justin McCarthy, "Same-Sex Marriage Support
    Reaches New High at 55%" (Gallup, accessed
    August 12, 2015), http://www.gallup.com/
    poll/169640/sex-marriage-support-reaches-new-
    high.aspx.

2   AT&T, "AT&T Recognized for Inclusion
    of Lesbian, Gay, Bisexual and Transgender
    Professionals in its Workforce" (May 16, 2011),
    http://www.att.com/gen/press-room?pid=19842&
    cdvn=news&newsarticleid=31922&mapcode=.

3   Joseph Farah, "Hollywood's Dual Standard Showing Again" (Los Angeles Times, July 13, 1993), http://articles.latimes.com/1993-07-13/local/me-12569_1_health-benefits.

4   The New York Times, "Disney Co. Will Offer Benefits to Gay Partners" (October 8, 1995), http://www.nytimes.com/1995/10/08/us/disney-co-will-offer-benefits-to-gay-partners.html.

5   The Economist, "Out and Proud" (August 29, 2002), http://www.economist.com/node/1302039.

6   National Gay & Lesbian Chamber of Commerce, Who We Are (accessed August 12, 2015), https://nglcc.org/who-we-are/founding-partners.

7   "UCC 'Firsts'" (accessed August 12, 2015), http://www.ucc.org/about-us_old-firsts.

8   Julia Duin, "Lutheran church to allow gay clergy, couples" (The Washington Times, August 22, 2009), http://www.washingtontimes.com/news/2009/aug/22/lutheran-church-to-allow-gay-clergy-couples/?page=all.

9   The CNN Wire Staff, "Presbyterian Church U.S.A. to allow gay and lesbian clergy" (CNN,

May 10, 2011), http://www.cnn.com/2011/US/05/10/presbyterian.gay.lesbian.ordination/.

10 Rowan Scarborough, "Pentagon holds first gay pride event" (The Washington Times, June 26, 2012) http://www.washingtontimes.com/news/2012/jun/26/pentagon-holds-first-gay-pride-event/?page=all.

11 Steve Tobak, "The Truth Behind Mozilla CEO Brendan Eich's Demise" (Fox Business, April 7, 2014), http://www.foxbusiness.com/technology/2014/04/07/truth-behind-mozilla-ceo-brendan-eichs-demise/.

12 Todd Starnes, "Atlanta Fire Chief: I was fired because of my Christian faith" (FoxNews.com, January 7, 2015), http://www.foxnews.com/opinion/2015/01/07/atlanta-fire-chief-was-fired-because-my-christian-faith.html.

13 Amanda Terkel, "Indiana Governor Signs Anti-Gay 'Religious Freedom' Bill At Private Ceremony" (Huffiest, March 26, 2015), http://www.huffingtonpost.com/2015/03/26/indiana-governor-mike-pence-anti-gay-bill_n_6947472.html.

14 9NEWS, "Denver mayor bans city-funded travel to Indiana" (April 1, 2015), http://www.9news.com/story/news/local/2015/03/31/denver-mayor-bans-city-funded-travel-to-indiana/70745780/.

15 CBS Local, "San Francisco Mayor Bans City Workers From Indiana Travel After Passage Of Religious Liberty Law" (March 26, 2015), http://sanfrancisco.cbslocal.com/2015/03/26/san-francisco-mayor-bans-city-workers-from-indiana-travel-after-passage-of-religious-liberty-law/.

16 Perry Stein, "D.C. mayor issues order banning city-funded travel to Indiana" (The Washington Post, March 31, 2015), http://www.washingtonpost.com/news/local/wp/2015/03/31/d-c-mayor-issues-order-banning-city-funded-travel-to-indiana/.

17 Alexandra Sifferlin, "Connecticut Bans State-Funded Travel to Indiana Over Controversial Law" (Time, March 30, 2015), http://time.com/3763622/connecticut-state-travel-indiana-religious-freedom-law/.

18 Phil Whaba, "Corporate America comes out swinging against 'religious freedom' laws"

(Fortune, March 31, 2015), http://fortune.com/2015/03/31/corporate-america-religious-freedom/.

19 Tim Evans, "Angie's List canceling Eastside expansion over RFRA" (IndyStar, April 2, 1015), http://www.indystar.com/story/money/2015/03/28/angies-list-canceling-eastside-expansion-rfra/70590738/.

20 USA Today, "Indiana governor signs amended 'religious freedom' law" (April 2, 2015), http://www.usatoday.com/story/news/nation/2015/04/02/indiana-religious-freedom-law-deal-gay-discrimination/70819106/.

Chapter One

21 Norman Geisler, *From God to Us* (Moody Press, 1974) 25–26.

22 Stephen Mansfield, *The Faith of Barack Obama* (Thomas Nelson Inc., 2011), 97.

23 Genesis 1:26–27; Romans 14:12

24 Lehman Strauss, "Marriage, Abortion and Divorce" (Bible.org, Accessed August 31, 2015),

https://bible.org/article/marriage-abortion-and-divorce.

25 CBS News/AP, "Montana man seeks license for second wife" (July 1, 2015), http://www.cbsnews.com/news/polygamous-montana-trio-applies-for-wedding-license/.

Chapter Two

26 http://www.cnsnews.com/news/article/terence-p-jeffrey/obama-state-union-same-sex-marriage-america-its-best

27 Phil Gast, "Obama announces he supports same-sex marriage" (CNN, May 9, 2012), http://www.cnn.com/2012/05/09/politics/obama-same-sex-marriage/.

28 Michael W. Chapman, "Men Celebrating Gay Marriage Ruling Spit on Catholic Priest" (CNS News, June 29, 2015), http://www.cnsnews.com/news/article/michael-w-chapman/men-celebrating-gay-marriage-ruling-spit-catholic-priest.

Chapter Three

29 Elizabeth M. Knowles, *The Oxford Dictionary of Quotations* (Oxford University Press, 2001), 215.

30 Todd Starnes, "'I am a follower of Christ': County clerk resigns rather than issue gay marriage licenses" (FoxNews.com, July 1, 2015), http://www.foxnews.com/opinion/2015/07/01/am-follower-christ-county-clerk-resigns-rather-than-issue-gay-marriage-licenses.html.

31 Supreme Court of the United States (Obergefell et all. v. Hodges, Director, Ohio Department of Health, et al., accessed August 19, 2015), http://www.supremecourt.gov/opinions/14pdf/14-556_3204.pdf, 28.

32 Supreme Court of the United States (Obergefell et all. v. Hodges, Director, Ohio Department of Health, et al., accessed August 19, 2015), http://www.supremecourt.gov/opinions/14pdf/14-556_3204.pdf, 7.

33 Michael Farris, "Flashback: Christian schools will have no choice about gay marriage" (USA Today, June 26, 2015), http://www.usatoday.com/story/opinion/2015/05/10/same-sex-marriage-christian-college-column/26883351/.

34 Michael Farris, "Flashback: Christian schools will have no choice about gay marriage" (USA Today, June 26, 2015), http://www.usatoday.com/story/opinion/2015/05/10/same-sex-marriage-christian-college-column/26883351/.

35 Mark Oppenheimer, "Now's the Time To End Tax Exemptions for Religious Institutions" (TIME, June 28, 2015), http://time.com/3939143/nows-the-time-to-end-tax-exemptions-for-religious-institutions/.

36 Jake New, "Keeping a Ban, Offering Support" (*Inside Higher Ed,* March 17, 2015), https://www.insidehighered.com/news/2015/03/17/gordon-college-maintains-ban-homosexual-practice-creates-human-sexuality-task-force.

37 Meg Bernhard and Mary Ellen McIntire, "What the Landmark Ruling on Gay Marriage Means for Higher Education" (The Chronicle of Higher Education, June 26, 2015), http://chronicle.com/article/What-the-Landmark-Ruling-on/231203/.

38 The Associated Press, "Baylor University drops 'homosexual acts' from conduct rules" (The Dallas Morning News, July 7, 2015), http://www.dallasnews.com/news/state/headlines/20150707-

baylor-university-drops-homosexual-acts-from-conduct-rules.ece.

39 Amy Biolchini, "Hope College to extend spousal benefits to gay couples after high court ruling" (HollandSentinel.com, July 5, 2015), http://www.hollandsentinel.com/article/20150705/NEWS/150709660.

40 Supreme Court of the United States (Obergefell et all. v. Hodges, Director, Ohio Department of Health, et al., accessed August 19, 2015), http://www.supremecourt.gov/opinions/14pdf/14-556_3204.pdf, 3.

41 Franklin Graham, quoted by Michael W. Chapman, "Rev. Graham on Gay Marriage Ruling: 'I Pray God Will Spare America From His Judgment'" (CNSNews, June 26, 2015), http://www.cnsnews.com/blog/michael-w-chapman/rev-graham-gay-marriage-ruling-i-pray-god-will-spare-america-his-judgment.

Chapter Five

42 Russell Moore, "Why the church should neither cave nor panic about the decision on gay

marriage" (The Washington Post, June 26, 2015), http://www.washingtonpost.com/news/acts-of-faith/wp/2015/06/26/why-the-church-should-neither-cave-nor-panic-about-the-decision-on-gay-marriage/.

Chapter Six

43 Christian Law Association, "Biblically Keeping the 'Main Thing' the 'Main Thing'" (Accessed August 19, 2015), http://www.christianlaw.org/cla/index.php/what-we-do/Initial_Response.

Chapter Seven

44 William L. Shirer, *The Rise and Fall of the Reich: A History of Nazi Germany* (Simon & Schuster, 2011), 249.

Chapter Nine

45 National Organization for Marriage, "National Organization for Marriage (NOM) Issues Statement Following US Supreme Court Decision on Marriage" (June 26, 2015), http://www.nomblog.com/40488/.

ABOUT THE AUTHOR

PAUL CHAPPELL is the senior pastor of Lancaster Baptist Church and president of West Coast Baptist College in Lancaster, California. His biblical vision has led the church to become one of the most dynamic Baptist churches in the nation. His preaching is heard on Daily in the Word, a daily radio broadcast heard across America. Dr. Chappell has been married to his wife Terrie for over thirty years, and they have four married children and eight grandchildren. His children are all serving in Christian ministry.

You can connect with Dr. Chappell through his blog, Twitter, and Facebook:

paulchappell.com
twitter.com/paulchappell
facebook.com/pastor.paul.chappell

Visit us online

strivingtogether.com

wcbc.edu